THE
POWER
OF THE
ROSARY

By Rev. Albert J. M. Shamon

THE RIEHLE FOUNDATION
Milford, Ohio 45150

Published by The Riehle Foundation

For additional copies write:
The Riehle Foundation
P.O. Box 7
Milford, Ohio 45150

ii

CONTENTS

The Rosary and Michelangelo

If ever you go to Rome, one of the sights you must see is the Sistine Chapel. Not too long ago, a group of Japanese artists cleaned away the dust and dirt of centuries beclouding Michelangelo's great frescos. Now after the clean-up job one can really appreciate the great genius of Michelangelo.

On the wall just above the main altar in the chapel, Michelangelo painted *The Last Judgment*. He finished this painting around 1541, while preparations were in progress for one of the greatest councils of the Church: the Council of Trent 1545.

This Council was to launch the counter-Reformation. As you know, in 1517, Martin Luther had revolted against the Church by denying certain doctrines. In the 1530's this revolt was in high gear, so plans for a General Council were in the making.

Michelangelo was an ardent son of the Church. He painted the Last Judgment to prepare the Church Fathers for the Council. The painting, in effect, was saying to the Bishops and Cardinals of the Council that they had better be very serious about what they were going to do, because God would judge their every word and action.

Michelangelo incorporated in the painting all those doctrines being challenged by the Protestant Reformers. The Reformers denied honor and devotion to Mary, the Mother of God.

So the artist put Mary in the place of honor in his painting, namely, at the right hand of her Son. Then just beneath her, Michelangelo painted a huge rosary hanging down over the ramparts of Heaven on which two souls are climbing up into Heaven. In this way, the great genius hoped to reflect his own devotion and that of the Church of the Renaissance to Mary and her rosary.

Just 30 years later (1571), the Turks under Selim the Sot, invaded Europe. Selim was the son of one of the greatest rulers of the Ottoman Empire, Suleiman the Magnificent. Suleiman had built a powerful army and navy, one of the greatest ever in the Empire. He was a wise man (Suleiman means Solomon); he never tried to invade Europe. But his son was not so wise. Drunk with the power he had inherited in 1566, Selim decided to invade Europe.

On the throne of Peter at this time happened to be a crusading Pope, St. Pius V. He called for a crusade against the Turks. Only a handful responded: Don John of Austria, the Spaniards, the Venetians, and the small

Papal fleet. They were no match for the Turkish fleet, which outnumbered them three to one. St. Pius V was a Dominican and Dominicans have a great devotion to the rosary. So Pius V called for a rosary crusade in Europe to help the Christian forces. On Oct. 7, 1571, the Christian forces under Don John and Andrea Doria met the Turks off the coast of Greece, the Gulf of Lepanto, and miraculously defeated them. Don John confessed that the victory was won, not by fighting arms, but by praying arms.

In thanksgiving for this victory, the Feast of the Most Holy Rosary was established on Oct. 7.

Also, to honor this great Dominican pope, St. Pius V, all succeeding Popes wear the white cassock of the Dominicans.

In the last apparition of Our Lady at Fatima, Oct. 13, 1917, Our Lady appeared as the Queen of the Holy Rosary. *In one hand she held the rosary and in the other the scapular.* Once she told St. Dominic that the rosary and the scapular would one day save the world. That day is today!

Blessed Virgin Mary to Saint Dominic, ''One Day through the Rosary and Scapular I will save the World''

~ 2 ~

A Thinking Prayer

To Father Gobbi, on October 7, 1983, Our Lady said:

> *Beloved sons, in the battle in which you are daily engaged against Satan and his crafty and dangerous seductions, and against the mighty armies of evil, apart from the special help given you by the angels of the Lord, it is necessary for you to employ a weapon which is both secure and invincible. This weapon is your prayer.*
>
> *...Prayer possesses a potent force and starts a chain reaction in good that is far more powerful than any atomic reaction.*

Now listen to this:

> *The prayer of my predilection is the holy rosary. For this reason, in my apparitions I always ask that it be recited... (#275).*

Why is the holy rosary so efficacious? There are many, many reasons.

One reason is that *the rosary is a thinking prayer.*

Bad thinking got us into the mess we are in today. For bad thinking spawned the French Revolution. Voltaire (1694-1778), Rousseau (1712-1778), Diderot (1713-1784),

4

and the Encyclopedists were the fathers of the French Revolution. Some of these men denied the existence of God. Or, if they admitted it, they held that God has nothing at all to do with this world; He wound it up like a clock and lets it run down. We are, so to speak, on our own. So, they glorified man and human reason. Their moral philosophy is called Deism and they labeled their times "The Age of the Enlightenment."

Their followers (the French revolutionaries), carrying their teachings out to their logical conclusion, murdered priests and sisters, pillaged and desecrated churches, smashed statues; they even enthroned Mademoiselle Aubryan, an actress, in the Cathedral of Notre Dame as goddess of reason.

This 18th century Deism bred 19th century Rationalism: and 19th century Rationalism gave birth to 20th century Secular Humanism in the United States and to Atheistic Communism in Russia. The Russian anarchist, Kropotkin, called the French Revolution "the source and origin of all the present Communist, anarchist, and socialist conceptions." Mikhail Gorbachev declared the spirit of the French Revolution present in the Soviet way of life (*Wall Street Journal*, 7/17/87).

In a word, the moral evils and errors of our day stem from the bad thinking that took root in France in the eighteenth century. That must be why the apparitions of Our Lady in the nineteenth century took place in France. Mary, the Mother of God, is our mother—truly our mother! This is not pious rhetoric. We are her children. She loves us dearly. She cares for us. When a child is in danger, its mother rushes to it. Mary saw the potential danger for her children of French Deism and Atheism so she went to the heart of the trouble: she circled France.

Apparitions of Our Lady in the 19th and 20th Centuries

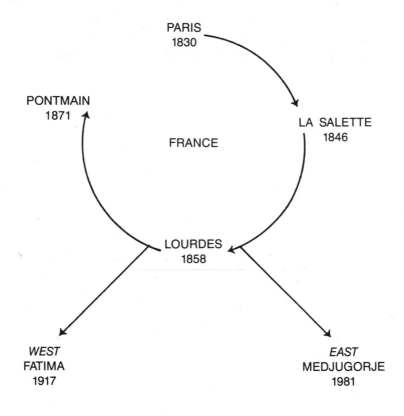

PARIS
1830

PONTMAIN
1871

LA SALETTE
1846

FRANCE

LOURDES
1858

WEST
FATIMA
1917

EAST
MEDJUGORJE
1981

PARIS, CATHERINE LABOURE

First, she started in the capital of France, *Paris*. On July 18, 1830, she appeared to a Charity nun, Catherine Laboure, in her convent on Rue du Bac (Baker Street), Paris. That same month, the July Revolution toppled the absolute monarchy of France and restored many of the principles of the French Revolution. The Church was once more vehemently attacked.

So in November of that same year, Our Lady gave Catherine Laboure a medal, depicting Mary as pouring out graces upon all. This medal became the instrument of so many miracles that people called it "the Miraculous Medal." Mary knew that a miracle was needed to bring France back to God.

LA SALETTE

Still, France did not come back to God. Mother Mary was not discouraged. Going clockwise from Paris, she next appeared September 19, 1846, to two children, Melanie and Maximin, at *La Salette* in southeastern France. She appeared there crying. She cried because people disregarded the holiness of Sunday and profaned the name of her Son. She cried, because, as she said, three-fourths of France would be lost to the Church and the other fourth would become lukewarm. Like a good mother, who tells her child not to play with fire, Mary warned that a terrible famine would happen if people did not return to God.

History labels 1848 "The Mad Year." In 1848 Karl Marx wrote his Communist Manifesto; Pope Pius IX had to flee from Rome to Gaeta for his life; his secretary, De Rossi, was stabbed to death; Wellington was called out of retirement to quell the riots in London; Metternich fled from Vienna for his life. And the potato famine came, taking over a million lives and causing Irish and Germans to emigrate in droves to America.

LOURDES

Our Lady's miracles, her tears, had been of little avail, so next she went to southern France, to Lourdes, February 11, 1858. There, to a little girl, Bernadette Soubirous, she revealed the two things needed to save France: penance and the rosary. Yet even so simple a request brought no national response. So the Franco-Prussian War began in 1871. Bismarck's mighty military juggernaut humbled the French armies. Paris was taken; and the victorious Germans swept westward planning to overtake France to the English Channel.

PONTMAIN

However, in western France lived the peasants of Normandy and Brittany, noted for their ardent Catholic faith. In the crisis, they turned to the Mother of God. On January 17, 1871, the Mother of God appeared to four children at Pontmain, about 180 miles west of Paris. Everyone prayed the rosary; and the children reported that each time they prayed the rosary, the image of Mary increased in size. Mary encouraged their prayer, saying, "Pray, my children, God will hear you in a short time. My Son permits Himself to be moved." They did as Mary asked: they prayed the rosary. And as if by magic, the westward sweep of the German armies halted. And within ten days an armistice was signed January 28, 1871. In gratitude to the Mother of God for her intervention, the French nation built the basilica of Our Lady at Pontmain.

In this apparition at Pontmain, Our Lady appeared surrounded by 43 stars. She was giving France 43 years to get its act together and return to God. Instead, France kept slipping further and further away from God. The schools were secularized and even an attempt was made to nationalize all Church property. Who will not give heed to the rudder must give heed to the rocks. Forty-three years from 1871 is 1914—the year the first World War began.

In the third year of this terrible war, the French Revolution spawned the Bolshevik Revolution in Russia. On April 16, 1917, Alexander Kerensky overthrew the Romanoff dynasty and gave Russia the only democratic government it had ever known. Kerensky, however, made the egregious blunder of trying to continue the war against Germany. Accordingly, General Ludendorf sent to Russia a boxcar of Bolsheviks—among them were Lenin, Trotsky and Stalin. On November 7, 1917, this handful overthrew Russia's democratic government. Kerensky fled to Australia, and Atheistic Communism won the resources that could implement worldwide aggression.

FATIMA

Yet within those fateful months of April and November, 1917, Our Lady left France and began appearing to the West at Fatima in Portugal, beginning with the Marian month of May 13, 1917, and ending with the Marian month of the rosary October 13, 1917. In every one of the six Fatima apparitions, the Mother of God gave mankind the antidote to the world poison of Atheistic Communism, namely, the rosary! In fact in the last apparition in October, Our Lady appeared as the Queen of the Most Holy Rosary.

"Pray the rosary daily" was her request. But again, few heeded it. So World War II followed.

MEDJUGORJE

Even after this horrendous war, the world did not seem to realize that its peace could be found only in God's will. So, as it was spinning merrily on its way to nuclear destruction, the Mother of God once more appeared—her last appearances! This time she appeared in the East, at Medjugorje in Yugoslavia, beginning June 24, 1981. For nine years she has been appearing to six children. And to four of them, she is still appearing daily as if to underscore the urgency of her message. As always, she is pleading for a return to God, especially through prayer—the prayer of the rosary. Only now she is asking us to pray all 15 decades daily.

THE ROSARY

Why this emphasis on the rosary? Our mother, the virgin most prudent, well knows that as we think, so we act. Creeds go before deeds. And she also knows that there is nothing so able to straighten out our thinking and counteract the errors of modern society as daily meditation on the mysteries of the rosary.

The rosary is good thinking. It drives home four great truths of religion.

1. The *Joyful Mysteries* of the rosary teach the first great truth of religion; namely, life and religion are meant to be joyful.

So many don't think that. Very often, they think the very opposite. George Eliot described some of the clergymen of her day as "pale faced mementos of solemnities." Glumdums!

The Joyful Mysteries teach the very opposite. They remind us that life is to be joyful; that religion, too, is to be joyful; that God has made us for happiness. That was why He put our first parents in a world that was a paradise. Did not Paul urge his beloved Philippians: "Rejoice in the Lord always. I shall say it again: rejoice!" (4:4).

But better still, the Joyful Mysteries tell us how we can obtain that joy; namely, by doing God's will as Mary and Joseph did, as Elizabeth and Zechariah did, as Anna and Simeon, the shepherds and the wise men did.

2. *The Sorrowful Mysteries* of the rosary teach the second great truth of religion; namely, sin is what makes this life a vale of tears.

The Sorrowful Mysteries tell us that sin—not doing God's will, but doing our will—is the path to sorrow. How few think it is! Youth, for instance, often think alcohol, drugs, and sex are the road to happiness. Going our way and not His way is the way to pain and unhappiness.

3. *The Glorious Mysteries* of the rosary teach the third great truth of religion; namely, life has a purpose, a goal beyond this life.

For the Christian, life is not cyclic: we are not going around in circles, like pagans. That is why the hallmark of the pagan is ennui, boredom, suicide. Purposeless activity can be maddening. If you had to throw a bowling ball down an alley with no pins, for just one evening, it would bore you to death. Put pins up, put purpose into the throwing, and it becomes an enjoyable game.

For the Christian, life is linear; we are going somewhere—to Heaven or to Hell.

The Glorious Mysteries emphasize that our destiny is Heaven; a glorious life beyond this life.

4. All 15 Mysteries of the rosary teach the fourth great truth of religion; namely, sanctity is for all and it is within the reach of all of us.

All 15 mysteries teach that great sanctity can be achieved

by ordinary people doing ordinary things, everyday, out of love for God, just as Mary and Joseph did.

In the eyes of the world, Joseph and Mary were just ordinary people. When Jesus awed his fellow townsmen by his eloquence, they asked, "Isn't this the son of Joseph?"—an ordinary carpenter! (*Lk.* 4:22). When Jesus claimed to be bread from Heaven, they again protested on the grounds that He came from ordinary folk. "Is this not Jesus, the son of Joseph? Do we not know his father and mother?" (*Jn.* 6:42)—just ordinary people! God doesn't ask us to be anything other than ordinary people—but good people whose one focus is Christ.

The rosary gets us thinking about such truths—and thinking leads to action. Our Lady knows that you cannot be thinking day in and day out on the mysteries of Our Lord's life and not be changed, for the thoughts that enfold you are the thoughts that mold you. Our Lady knows that. Hence her ardent requests for our saying the rosary.

Our Lady does not ask for Revolution (which is only a change of structures); for changing structures changes nothing. Overthrowing the monarchy of France did not better the nation. Overthrowing the Romanov dynasty and the Kerensky government for Communism did not help Russia. Toppling the regime of Batista for Castro did not save Cuba. What Our Lady seeks—and the Church and the gospel—is Renewal, which is a change of hearts. That is why she asks for the rosary, for the rosary renews hearts, changes people; and when people change, society will change.

~ 3 ~

My Mind Wanders

One of the greatest objections to the rosary is precisely because it is a thinking prayer. Some will say, "I don't like to think." Or "I can't concentrate on the mysteries. My mind wanders. That's why I quit saying the rosary."

I think the trouble here is that too often we try to intellectualize the mysteries. We peer into them to extract lessons from them. Rather, we should just look at the mysteries of the rosary in the Ignatian sense of contemplation. St. Ignatius said, just look at the scenes of Our Lord's life without trying to pull out all kinds of lessons and applications to your life. Just be there, like watching the TV series *"You were there."* The lessons and applications will come spontaneously.

Haven't you gone to a movie and have a friend ask how you liked it? As you gave your answer, you were unconsciously analyzing the picture. Without even being aware of it, you were drawing conclusions about the picture just by looking at the movie.

So in the rosary. Just look at the scenes of Our Lord's life with Our Lady for the length of 10 Hail Marys. Like a movie, they will begin to say something to you without your having to do anything but look. While you are looking at the scenes, God is working in your heart.

One day I was saying the Glorious Mysteries. I was thinking of the second one: the Ascension. The thought just surfaced of how (at the Ascension) the apostles were being left all alone—but with Mary. I wondered how those eleven ordinary men could change the world.

Then out of the blue I began thinking of Our Lady's apparitions to young children at Lourdes, Fatima, and Medjugorje. I thought they were just a few kids and yet they affected so many millions. At Medjugorje I thought of the 15 million who have already been touched.

Then it became quite clear to me of how much greater impact must the apostles have had, for they not only had seen Christ, they had been with Him for years. Then, too, the Mother of God was their companion for over 15 years after His Ascension. Wow! Before I could go on, I was on the third mystery.

Last year (1989), I made my priest's retreat at Putnam, Connecticut. Eileen George conducted the retreat. Eileen is the mother of eight and has terminal cancer. She is an extraordinary ordinary person, very gifted by God the Father, whom she calls "Daddy."

Through some fluke of not advertising the retreat, only eleven priests were there. For us that was a break. Each night, after the last conference, we would all go down to the cafeteria for a snack and then sit around Eileen asking her all kinds of questions about the Father, the Son and the Holy Spirit, about Heaven, Hell, Purgatory, about the Mass, the priesthood, the Church, good and evil in the world. And she was so gracious. She talked to us as a mother to ones she loved. And she shared with us, her marvelous experiences with the Trinity, strengthening our faith and deepening our love and appreciation for the Church and our priesthood.

Well, one evening after our little session, I went to the

chapel to finish my 15 decades of the rosary. When I came to the third Glorious Mystery, the Descent of the Holy Spirit, all I could think about was that our little group of priests around Eileen was like the apostles around Mary. And as Eileen inspired us priests with a greater love and understanding of Jesus, Mary must have done the same thing, only on a far deeper scale, for the apostles. It became so clear to me how Mary was truly the Mother of the Church, and the central part she must play in every priest's life.

Another time I was thinking about the first Sorrowful Mystery, the Agony in the Garden. I was picturing Jesus leaving the Last Supper room with His eleven and going down the steps that lead to the Kidron valley and to Gethsemane. Around that time I was also thinking of how I had an appointment to go to the IRS for an auditing of some tax returns. Well, whichever way you cut it, that gives one a scary, uncomfortable feeling. Then the thought spontaneously surfaced of how Jesus must have felt in going to Gethsemane: He was going to face death, a horrible death, marked by excruciating pain and ignominy. With the IRS interview hanging over my head, I could empathize in some small way with the inner feelings He must have experienced.

Then another thought arose of its own accord: see what Jesus was doing. He was going to the Garden to pray. That was how He was going to meet the situation—with prayer! Then I thought to myself that is how I ought to confront every trial in my own life—by prayer. This mystery in Our Lord's life confirmed my resolve to pray always when face to face with a problem.

Another time when I was meditating on the second

Joyful Mystery, the Visitation, the thought surfaced of the role of women in the redemption. It struck me that the first people who were in on the secrets of God were women: Mary and Elizabeth. Both Joseph and Zechariah were really on the outside looking in. The women led the men. I told that to some priest, and commented how can anyone ever say that women in the Church are second-class citizens. This quick-witted priest quipped, ''The babes in their wombs were men.''

Well, anyway, I hope you see what I mean. If you just look, almost leisurely, at the scenes of Our Lord's life, you will reap fruit you never suspected. For our sights, God will give us insight.

The ten Hail Marys are like background music while you are watching Our Lord's life. Background music helps us when reading or working. We don't pay much attention to the music, but it helps us. So in reciting the Hail Marys, you don't pay much attention to them; they are the background music to help us contemplate the mysteries of Our Lord's life.

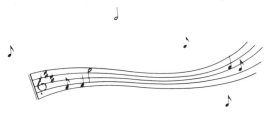

Hail Mary, full of grace. . .

~ 4 ~

Too Repetitious

An objection to the rosary brought up by some adults is that the rosary is too repetitious.

Psychologists tell us that the same formula repeated over and over again has a tranquilizing effect. Rhythmic repetition soothes the mind. That is why counting sheep—the rhythmic repetition of numbers—can lull to sleep. Knitting—rhythmic action—was one of the therapies used for shell-shocked soldiers in World War I. The rosary—the rhythmic repetition of the fifty Hail Marys— can soothe the mind and tranquilize it, thus freeing it so that it can think on the mysteries.

Once a young lady told Archbishop Fulton J. Sheen that she would never say the rosary, for anyone who keeps saying the same thing over and over again can't be sincere. The Archbishop asked her if she were engaged. She answered Yes.

"Does your fiance love you?"

"Of course."

"How do you know?"

"He told me so."

"Did he just tell you once?"

"Of course not."

"Did he tell you twice?"

"He's told me a hundred times that he loves me."

"Oh, I wouldn't marry him. He can't be sincere—saying the same thing over and over again."

When people are in love, they say so—not once, but a hundred times over, again and again and again.

The truth is, repetition is the language of love. Repetition does not create monotony; in fact it creates stability; it reaffirms; even serves as a cushion against the future shock of change. When a mother says to her child, "I love you," the child wants to hear it again and again.

Monotony is eliminated, not by constant change, but by attention and sincerity and purpose. If golf were only hitting a ball, it would be worse than monotonous. But give it purpose; have a green and a cup to shoot for, ah, then it becomes a wonderful game.

The most essential functions of life are repetitive: eating is repetitive; sleeping is repetitive; working is repetitive; loving is repetitive. The rosary is the language of love.

I think the following news clipping from the Rochester *Democrat and Chronicle* (1/24/54) says it all.

'I Love You' Girl adds 'I Do'

New York—UP—A girl who baffled the Chinese Communists for two years by saying nothing but "I love you" over and over again in 400 letters to her prisoner sweetheart in Korea added a two-word postscript yesterday.

She said "I do."

Theresa MacDonald, 21, and Cpl. William C. Rhatigan, 22, were married in the Church of the Fourteen Holy Martyrs in Brooklyn.

An estimated 500 persons witnessed the ceremony, which came after a long romance. The couple became engaged on Christmas Day, 1950. A few months later, Rhatigan left for Korea with the Second Infantry Division.

He was captured in May, 1951, and released last year. During his imprisonment, he received a steady stream of letters saying nothing but "I love you." Not one of the letters was halted by the censors.

"Those letters certainly had the Chinese puzzled." Rhatigan said, *"but they didn't puzzle me any. It was all I wanted to hear, and Theresa knew it."*

Power of the Rosary: for Persons

Roberta Panek is a part-time x-ray technician and mother of four children. She used to write a column titled "Just another day." One article she titled "Praying rosary becomes a form of bonding." That was another way of putting Fr. Peyton's slogan: "The Family that prays together stays together." The article began:

> Tonight, my 8-year-old daughter, Laura, and I did something different. We prayed the rosary together. It was great! From 7:35 to 7:55 p.m. we prayed the Glorious Mysteries and it was indeed glorious! At one point during our praying, we sat and smiled at each other. We smiled and smiled. Our hearts were merging. . .
>
> Two days lapsed. . .Laura and I have prayed the rosary for three days in a row. It's bonding for us. I appreciate and savor this time. . .
>
> Praying makes us more conscious of the present. Everything that we do (say, eat, drink, think, write) has some small effect on our future. Little decisions can even be as significant as big ones. Praying helps us to direct our thoughts. . .

The family needs cementing today. Roberta says that the rosary is the cement. Our Lady has been asking for the family rosary, for it will keep the family a family. I have been promoting a National Rosary Crusade against abortion. Last May, 1989, a lady wrote this letter:

> *Dear Father Shamon,*
>
> *God bless you for "preaching" the rosary! We need this powerful prayer to cure so many ills and I think it is wonderful that you are using Our Lady's weapon against abortion.*
>
> *The Rosary brought me back to the sacraments after 15 years. The Rosary converted my Jewish husband who has since died, may he rest in peace; but I am so grateful. He loved Our Lady, his "Jewish Mother." And it was a true miracle of conversion.*
>
> *The Rosary brought my sister back to the sacraments after 10 years.*
>
> *Our Lady through her Rosary, meditating on Our Lord's life, brings us back to Jesus and Reconciliation with Him in the sacrament of confession and the celebration of the Eucharist.*
>
> *I agree with you, it is our weapon against the murder of the unborn... So I will, with God's help, offer 15 decades a week for your Crusade against abortion.*
>
> *God bless you.*

At Sodus Point, overlooking Lake Ontario, stands a historic Catholic church. Bishop Bernard J. McQuaid, the first bishop of Rochester, New York, named it St. Rose of Lima to honor *Rose Lummis* (1844-1900), who had deeded the property and the building, Lummis Hall, for use as a Catholic Church.

At the age of 21, Rose had entered the Catholic Church. In her zeal for her new-found faith, she converted her Episcopalian minister, the Rev. William P. Salt. He became a priest and Vicar General of the Diocese of Newark and Rector of Seton Hall. Rose wanted to be a Sister, but poor health prevented this. So she became an Associate Member of the Society of the Sacred Heart, Canada, taking the vows of religion. And she spent her fortune and her life serving the disadvantaged and needy.

Rose had a great love for the rosary. She prayed the rosary publicly every day at 3:00 P.M. Her life is filled with incidents of the power of that rosary. When she wanted a church and a resident priest for the little village of Port Dover on Lake Erie, she prayed a decade of her rosary each day; and, what everyone thought would never happen happened: Dover got a church and pastor.

Rose worked not only in Canada, but also in the South, from her headquarters in Hendersonville, North Carolina.

One Sunday afternoon, the area doctor came to Rose and asked that she send a priest to one of his patients dying in the Blue Ridge Mountains. The man was a poor worker from New England, who had come to the South to battle tuberculosis.

Because it was Sunday, Rose knew that Father Marion would be home at Asheville. On any other day, there would have been little or no chance of reaching him, for the pastor would have been on horseback visiting his parishioners over a 140 mile area. But it was Sunday, so Rose sent a telegram to Asheville for him, and happily Father received it. He arrived the next morning by train to Hendersonville and headed immediately for the mountains, accompanied by a Mr. McKenna, who knew something of the roads higher up.

The doctor had left some pine boughs on the road to guide them to their obscure destination. Mile after mile, they journeyed slowly upwards off the main road. When they came to the doctor's sign almost buried in the underbrush, they passed through a gap in the mountains and clambered straight down until they came on a solitary cabin without sign of habitation. They entered the yard, opened the door, but there was no sign of life anywhere—only two unmade beds in a half-empty room. Father thought, "He must have died and everybody must be at the cemetary."

However, Father went into another room and exclaimed, "God help him, poor fellow; here he is!"

They had found the poor man, lying helpless and suffering, with flies covering his emaciated face, for he was too weak to brush them off. The dying man recognized the priest and he looked up with a faint, welcoming smile.

"I knew you would come to me, Father," he said with a gasping sob, but satisfied that now he could receive the last sacraments. When Father asked the dying man if he were resigned, he raised himself with effort and said, "I am, Father; I want to go now." Father stayed until sunset, then reluctantly left for Tryon, to spend the night.

The next morning, a messenger came in time to prevent Father from boarding the train to Asheville with the news that the sick man had died last night. Father borrowed a horse and hurried back up the mountains. At high noon he arrived. A few men loitered around the door of the cabin and looked at him curiously as he dismounted, tired, hot and dusty. The good woman of the house came forward with a rough, but sincere, welcome. "Put the critter in the barn, and I'll push hay through the cracks." She then invited the priest into the cabin to dinner, and he sat down with the family.

After dinner, they led him to the dead man, whom they had laid out in his best clothes, as respectfully and reverently as if he were their very own. Father was much moved; it said so much for these people, who might have buried the stranger coffinless and concealed his belongings.

The woman brought forth an old leather bag, the property of the dead man. It was almost empty, but contained a book by St. Francis de Sales, well worn, and a few odds and ends, all of which Father presented to the family.

"And now," the woman said anxiously, "there ought to be a watch, for he had a chain about him that he loved mighty well. I've looked a right smart for that 'ere watch, but I can't find it."

"Let me see the chain," Father asked.

Slowly and solemnly the woman went into another room, and came back with a pillbox, which she opened with great care, holding the contents up to Father. He looked down on the poor, worn, blackened chain; it was the dead man's rosary! Seeing the priest's earnest look, the woman repeated: "He loved it mighty well!" Father took it up reverently.

"We'll bury it with him."

"Yes," said the woman again; "he loved it mighty well."

Together they went to the dead man, and the woman put the rosary on as if it were really a watch chain.

I cannot tell you how deeply touched I was when I read that story. It showed me to what lengths the Mother of God will go to help her children who love the rosary. The dead man "loved the rosary mighty well"; countless times he had prayed "Holy Mary, Mother of God, pray for me now and at the hour of my death." And she did: her prayers brought her Son to him at the hour of his death. What a grace!

When Rose Lummis herself was dying, Delia Gleason, her biographer, wrote: "It was the rosary that cheered her passing moments. It was always with her, to be drawn out the instant she was alone, in the train, driving or walking, one always noticed it tenderly clasped or quietly passing through her fingers. She prayed always...''

One day, *Dr. Carlos Finlay* returned home very late at night. He was tired and sleepy, when he remembered that he had not said his rosary that day. He always prayed the rosary daily. So he devoutly began to say his rosary. A buzzing mosquito flew persistently around his head, forcing him to divert his attention many times.

Suddenly, as if inspired by the Blessed Virgin, to whom he was addressing his prayer, the idea, which made him famous, came into his mind that the mosquito is the transmitting agent of yellow fever and malaria. He acted on this theory and proved it to be correct. This concluded a long series of efforts and investigations by numerous scientists for an answer to malaria. Thus was the way paved for the completion of the Panama Canal.

The great Austrian composer, *Franz Haydn*, told his admirers: "When, in the course of composing a work, I feel myself bogged and get no inspiration, I take my beads and start praying the rosary. Soon my mind becomes loaded with so many melodies that I am able to notate but a few only."

Frederick Ozanan, founder of the St. Vincent de Paul Society for giving spiritual and material help to the poor, was an unbeliever when young. One day he entered a church in Paris. It was empty except for an old man, praying the rosary in front of an altar. He went near to get a closer look at this man and discovered that it was his professor Ampere who was saying the rosary.

Ampere was a great mathematician and physicist who created the science of electro-dynamics and invented among other things the means of sending telegraphic messages. Yet Ampere prayed the rosary so devoutly that Ozanan was convinced that the religion which Ampere followed was true. Later, after his conversion to the Catholic faith, Ozanan often said: "The rosary of Ampere did me more good than all the books and sermons." Ozanan is now up for beatification.

Maryknoll *Bishop James E. Walsh* in a letter to Father Paul R. Milde, O.S.B., described how saying the rosary sustained and consoled him during his years of confinement in a Chinese prison.

"My great support during twelve years of imprisonment was the rosary. I had no religious books and could not obtain any, so it was impossible for me to celebrate Mass or recite the Breviary.

"Privation is the keynote of prison life. With no facilities on hand except air to breathe and bare walls to contemplate, the situation appears gloomy. No place to go...nothing to do...endless monotony to look forward to...the prospect is bleak. What to do under these conditions? From long habit the answer with me was prompt and automatic. Turn to the rosary of course. Fall back on the rosary.

"It can be said on your ten fingers as easily as if you had the beads. To say the rosary one needs nothing at all but time; and now I had plenty of that...Instead of just worrying about people all day long...you can help them with the rosary...

"My great, constant, every-present companion was the rosary. It ministered to my deepest need...Its fifteen mysteries provided a clear and complete review of the great central truths of religion...

"The rosary sustained me when other means were lacking. It came to my aid whenever I felt oppressed by any trouble. It was my never-failing lifeline all through my prison years."

One of the great generals of World War I was Marshal *Ferdinand Foch.* His mother was a companion of St.

Bernadette of Lourdes. Together with Bernadette, she always prayed the rosary at the cave at Massabielle. She taught Ferdinand to have a special love for Mary and her rosary. "Always," she used to tell him, "be faithful to your rosary. Never let a day go by without reciting it devoutly." Each evening they recited it together.

When World War I broke out, her son led the armies of France, and his great victories were in no small part due to his fidelity to praying the rosary every day. He died grasping his rosary.

In *Our Sunday Visitor* I spotted a notice of how the Rosary had brought a priest back to his priesthood. "Attributing his readmission to the priesthood to the Rosary, Father William Blazewicz stood before his congregation at Sacred Heart Parish in Mondovi, Wis., and told them his story of losing his faith and regaining it." (5/14/89).

Oh, the power of the rosary! It has such power, not only because thinking on the mysteries of Our Lord's life can change us, but especially because Mary makes the rosary her prayer and prays with us.

When in each Hail Mary we say, "Holy Mary, Mother of God, pray for us sinners. . ." Mary accedes to our request and joins her prayers to ours thus making the rosary most powerful. As she told Fr. Gobbi once, "You ask me to pray for you fifty times. I hear your prayer and pray with you. And so your prayer becomes all powerful, for my Son will deny me nothing."

St. Louis de Montfort wrote:

> *If you say the rosary faithfully until death, I do assure you that, in spite of the gravity of your sins, 'you shall receive a never fading crown of glory.'*

Even if you are on the brink of damnation, even if you have one foot in Hell, even if you have sold your soul to the devil. . . sooner or later you will be converted and will amend your life and save your soul. IF—and mark well what I say—IF YOU SAY THE ROSARY DEVOUTLY EVERY DAY OF YOUR LIFE. . ." (p. 12).

The saints have called the daily praying of the rosary a sign of predestination to Heaven. And the writings of the saints contain no doctrinal error.

~ 6 ~

Power of the Rosary: for Nations

Our Lady repeatedly has told us that peace will come only through a return to God through prayer, especially the prayer of the rosary. But so many still do not listen to her message. So, action speaks louder than words. Outlined below are a few facts, of what Mary has done in Japan, Austria, Brazil, Russia and the United States ought to have a cumulative force that should move all Catholics to start praying the rosary daily and, if possible, as a family.

1. *Our Lady speaks to Japan: the rosary of Hiroshima.*

At 2:45 a.m. on August 6, 1945, a B-29 took off from the island of Tinian to drop the first atomic bomb on Japan. At 8:15 a.m. the bomb exploded eight city blocks from the Jesuit Church of Our Lady's Assumption in Hiroshima. Half a million people were wiped out. All that was left was darkness, blood, burns, moans, fire and spreading terror.

However, the church and the four Jesuit fathers stationed there survived: Fathers Hugo Lassalle, Kleinsorge, Cieslik and Schiffer. According to the experts they "ought to be dead," being as they were within the most deadly one-mile radius of the explosion. Nine days later on August 15, Feast of Our Lady's Assumption, peace came.

The miracle of their survival, their devotion to Our Lady, their church dedicated to her Assumption, made it clear to these survivors that this was more than coincidence. It taught them the power of Mary and her prayer, the rosary. So their response to the atom bomb was to launch a Rosary Crusade for peace in Japan.

Think of the power of a river. It is made up of tiny drops of water, numberless tiny drops of rain. Together these tiny drops make the mighty river, which can carry heavy ships and change arid deserts into fruitful farms and gardens.

So, too, the Rosary Crusade, the rosaries of countless persons all over the world become an immense and irresistable spiritual force for peace.

2. *Austria: the miracle of the Russian pullout.*

At the end of World War II, the allies did a nasty thing: they turned Catholic Austria over to the Russians. The Austrians tolerated this Soviet domination for three years, but that was enough. They wanted the Soviets out of their country. But what could Austria do: seven million against 220,000 million?

Then a priest, Pater Petrus, remembered Don John of Austria. Outnumbered three to one, Don John led the Papal, Venetian, and Spanish ships against the Turks at Lepanto, and through the power of the rosary miraculously defeated them. So Pater Petrus called for a rosary crusade against the Soviets. He asked for a tithe: that ten percent of the Austrians, 700,000, would pledge to say the rosary daily for the Soviets to leave their country. 700,000 pledged.

For seven years the Austrians prayed the rosary. Then, on May 13, the anniversary of the apparition at Fatima, in 1955, the Russians left Austria.

Even to this day military strategists and historians are baffled. Why did the Communists pull out? Austria is a strategically located country, a door to the West, rich in mineral deposits and oil reserves? To them it was an enigma.

Al Williams, former custodian of the National Pilgrim Statue of Our Lady of Fatima, heard me tell this story once. He said to me, "You know, Father, I am Austrian. Well, three months before Therese Neumann died, I visited her (June 18, 1962). One question I asked her was, 'Why did the Russians leave Austria?' She told me, 'Verily, verily, it was the rosaries of the Austrian people.' "

In other words, Our Lady's rosary did what the Hungarian Freedom Fighters could not do with a bloodbath of 25,000 people. John Cortes, brilliant writer and diplomat of the 19th century wrote: "Those who pray do more for the world than those who fight. If the world is going from bad to worse, it is because there are more battles than prayers."

3. *Brazil:* **Why not the way of Cuba?**

In the November, 1964, issue of the Reader's Digest, there was a story titled: "The Country that Saved Itself." That country was Brazil. The stage was all set in 1961 to take over Brazil, just like Cuba. But guess who thwarted this Communist takeover? The women of Brazil with their rosaries! "Without the women," said one of the leaders of the counterrevolution, "we could never have halted Brazil's plunge toward communism."

One night in mid-1962, Dona Amelia Bastos listened to her husband and a band of anti-Reds discuss the looming threat of Communism. "I suddenly decided," she said, "that politics had become too important to be left entirely to the men. . . Moreover, who has more at stake in what's happening to our country than we women?"

She formed CAMDE (Campaign of Women for Democracy). In Belo Horizonte, 20,000 women reciting the rosary aloud broke up the leftist meeting there. In Sao Paulo, 600,000 women praying the rosary in one of the most moving demonstrations in Brazilian history, sounded the death knell of the Communist revolution.

These women with rosaries in their hands or around their necks, issued a 1300 word proclamation:

> *This nation which God has given us, immense and marvelous as it is, is in extreme danger. We have allowed men of limitless ambition, without Christian faith or scruples, to bring our people misery, destroying our economy, disturbing our social peace, to create hate and despair. They have infiltrated our nation, our government, our armed forces and even our churches...*
>
> *Mother of God, preserve us from the fate and suffering of the martyred women of Cuba, Poland, Hungary and other enslaved nations!*

Sounds like the United States, doesn't it? Our Lady at Fatima said that if her requests were not heard that the errors of Russia would spread over all the world even to the United States. Well, it has happened here. Whoever would have believed that Americans would have defended the right to murder unborn children, to hold up homosexuality as an alternate lifestyle? That the Supreme Court of our nation would outlaw God from our schools, legitimize hard-core pornography, and so on and on.

And who has more at stake here than the women of our nation? Please God, may they, like the women of Brazil, take the lead in getting our country back from the forces that would destroy it. And may they use the weaponry, recommended by Our Lady, and used by the women of Brazil: the rosary! Not just the private rosary, but the family rosary, for it is the family that is threatened.

4. *Our Lady speaks to Russia.*

a. *On October 13, 1960.*

Most of us remember the time when Nikita Khrushchev visited the United Nations in October, 1960 and boasted that "they would bury us"—would annihilate us! And to emphasize his boasting, he took off his shoe and pounded the desk before the horrified world assembly.

This was no idle boast. Khrushchev knew his scientists had been working on a nuclear missile and had completed their work and planned on November 1960, the 43rd anniversary of the Bolshevik Revolution, to present it to Khrushchev.

But here's what happened. Pope John XXIII had opened and read the third Fatima secret given to Sister Lucy. He authorized the Bishop of Leiria (Fatima) to write to all the bishops of the world, inviting them to join with the pilgrims of Fatima on the night of October 12-13, 1960, in prayer and penance for Russia's conversion and consequent world peace.

On the night of October 12-13, about a million pilgrims spent the night outdoors in the Cova da Iria at Fatima in prayer and penance before the Blessed Sacrament. They prayed and watched despite a penetrating rain which chilled them to the bone.

At the same time at least 300 dioceses throughout the world joined with them. Pope John XXIII sent a special blessing to all taking part in this unprecedented night of reparation.

Well, here is what happened. On the night between October 12 and 13, right after his shoe-pounding episode, Khrushchev suddenly pulled up stakes and enplaned

in all haste for Moscow, cancelling all subsequent en-
gagements. Why?

Marshall Nedelin, the best minds in Russia on nuclear
energy and several government officials were present for
the final testing of the missile that was going to be
presented to Khrushchev. When countdown was completed, the missile, for some reason or other, did not
leave the launch pad. After 15 or 20 minutes, Nedelin
and all the others came out of the shelter. When they
did, the missile exploded killing over 300 people. This
set back Russia's nuclear program for 20 years, prevented
all-out atomic warfare, the burying of the U.S.—and this
happened on the night when the whole Catholic world
was on its knees before the Blessed Sacrament, gathered
at the feet of our Rosary Queen in Fatima. Our Lady
does not want nuclear war.

b. *On May 13, 1984.*

On May 13, 1984, one of the largest crowds ever was
gathered at Fatima to celebrate the anniversary of the
first apparition of Our Lady there. On that very day a
massive explosion destroyed two-thirds of the surface-
to-air and ship-to-ship missiles of the Soviet Union's
mightiest fleet—the Northern Fleet, charged in wartime
with cutting off NATO's Atlantic sea lanes. According
to *Jane's Defense Weekly* of London, this was "the greatest
disaster to occur in the Soviet Navy since World War II."
Is it not time that we place more confidence in the
promises and power of Our Lady?

c. *On April 28, 1986.*

Everyone has read of the Chernobyl disaster in the
Ukraine. Direct damage was about 2.7 billion dollars.
The indirect cost was far more, with the contamination
of 1,000 square miles of farmland. But the greatest effect

was the spiritual effect on the Russian people.

A prominent Russian writer pointed out that Chernobyl is the Ukrainian word for "wormwood" (a bitter herb used as a tonic in rural Russia). Then he observed that in the Book of Revelation, it is written that a great star fell from the heavens making a third part of the waters bitter. And the name of that star is Wormwood (*Rev.* 8:10-11).

With uncanny speed this connection between the Chernobyl disaster and the words of Revelation has spread across Russia, giving Chernobyl the quality of an almost supernatural disaster. It has had an impact on the Russian people, especially when they remembered that Christianity came to the very region of Chernobyl to the tribe of Rus in 998 A.D.

d. On May 12, 1988.

On May 18, 1988, the Associated Press reported that "Blast shuts Soviet's sole missile motor plant." The article began, "A major explosion has shut down the only plant in the Soviet Union that makes the main rocket motors of that country's newest long-range nuclear missile, according to U.S. officials." The Pentagon issued a statement saying it happened May 12 and "destroyed several buildings at a Soviet propellant plant in Pavlograd," about 500 miles southwest of Moscow in the Ukraine.

Just before that, on May 3, 1988, here in our own country, an explosion ripped apart a Nevada plant that was probably handling the ammonium perchlorate used in the main rocket motor for the SS-24. Again, is not Our Lady preventing nuclear war, in response to our rosaries of reparation?

5. Our Lady Speaks to the U.S.

Heaven always accommodates itself to our limitations.

On the first Christmas, to speak to shepherds, God used angels; to speak to the wise men, He used a star; and to speak to the United States, He used our ordinary instrument of communication, the weekly magazine—He used *Newsweek*, June 12, 1989 and *U.S. News*, August 7, 1989.

In the June 12 issue of *Newsweek*, there is a story about atomic help given by Americans to friendly nations. Laws forbid our sharing sensitive information with other nations. American scientists skirt this law with France by a name called "Negative Guidance."

For instance, when the French were trying to develop multiple independently targeted warheads, the Americans let them know by indirection whether or not they were getting hot or cold.

If the French said, "We tried that but it didn't work," the Americans would answer, "There are other ways."

The French would ask, "Other ways?" And the questions would go on till the right answer was reached.

In the June 12 article, *Newsweek* showed a picture of the French testing of the atomic bomb in the Pacific.* Underneath the photo is this caption: "Other ways? *French test on the Pacific island of Mururoa?*"

In the photo, one can spot very clearly the image of Our Lord crucified and of Our Lady. The image of the crucified Lord is in the red fire of the bomb. But to His right in white light (in the cloud of the explosion) is the outline of Our Lady. She is there as if to answer the question: "Other ways?" Her answer is, "Yes, there are other ways besides atomic war. It is my way: the way of the rosary."

---

* See back cover. AFP photo courtesy of Black Star.

In physics we learned that white fire is hotter than red. Our Lady is in white in contrast to the fiery red of the atomic mushroom. It is Mary's dramatic way of saying now, as once she did at Fatima when the sun twirled miraculously and danced Oct. 13, 1917: "God is more powerful than any atomic bomb. You want peace? Well, it is in my hands and not in bombs, atomic or nuclear. There are other ways, indeed, my way—the way of the mother of all mankind."

In *U.S. News and World Report* (August 7, 1989), that same atomic bomb photo reappeared twice with an article "America's Doomsday Project." It was subtitled "The U.S. has a secret survival plan in the event of nuclear war." What a sense of humor Our Lady has! She seems to be saying, "There *are* other ways. Yes, there is a secret survival plan for the U.S.—it is turning to me in prayer, the prayer of the rosary."

On August 14, 1989, a Japanese scientist took his geiger counter to Apparition Hill in Medjugorje to register the radioactivity there. It read 10, which is normal. When Our Lady became present on the Hill at 10:30 p.m., it registered 300,000—the equivalent to the center of a nuclear bomb.

Again, Our Lady is saying, "I am just as powerful as any nuclear bomb. You Americans put too much trust in your own resources. You think the bomb is the answer—your technology! It is not! Put your trust, not in the bomb; the bomb will destroy. There is another way—Me! Put your trust in me! I will bring peace!"

On October 13, 1988, the 71st anniversary of the last apparition of Our Lady at Fatima, through Fr. Gobbi, she reminded her priests of that apparition by repeating part of the message there: "I am the Queen of the Holy

Rosary and I bless you all with this sign of my sure victory (*Our Lady Speaks to Her Beloved Priests*, #391). Her sign of sure victory is the rosary. She promised it at Fatima; and she reiterated it there 71 years later.

> . . .*frequently recite the holy rosary! Then the powerful Red Dragon will be shackled by this chain, and his margin of action will become ever more restricted. In the end he will be left impotent and harmless.*
>
> *The miracle of the triumph of my Immaculate Heart will be made manifest to all.*
>
> (To Fr. Gobbi 10/7/83)

And it is being made manifest in the collapse of Communism in Eastern Europe. How else can we explain this incredible phenomenon? It is not the military, not the politicians, not the media that is bringing this about. It is the millions upon millions of people responding to Our Lady's requests at Fatima, at Medjugorje, etc., who are making this happen—the ordinary people!—their sacrifices, their prayers, their rosaries!

~ Appendix 1 ~

The Rosary:
Weapon For Peace
(Weapon Against Abortion)

The most effective weapon against abortion is prayer, and particularly THE ROSARY, public and private. It can save lives and convert the American people. The public Rosary should be (and often is) the prayer of the Pro-Life Movement.

Abortion is not just a legal problem. It is a moral one. "We must obey God rather than men" (*Acts* 5:29). It will be resolved when the American people return to their Judeo-Christian values. Only God can accomplish this conversion, and He will if we ask Him in prayer.

For the last two years, I have been promoting the perpetual rosary crusade, asking people to pledge one hour a week to pray the 15 decades of the Rosary for the overturn of abortion. The response has been wonderful, and the graces and successes apparent.

We wish to expand on that theme and crusade for ROSARIES FOR PEACE.

The Rosary is the wonder weapon. At Lepanato in 1571, it sank ships. In 1955, it removed the Russians from Catholic Austria. In 1962, it prevented the Communist takeover of Brazil. In the 1980's, it has been documented that the bloodless revolution which removed Ferdinand Marcos from power in the Phillippines was largely attributed to the praying of the Rosary.

THE ROSARY IS THE WEAPON THAT CAN BRING PEACE TO THE WORLD. (Our Lady explicitly said this at Fatima.)

TO TURN THE TIDE OF EVIL IN AMERICA, IN THE WORLD, A TITHE OF ROSARIES SHOULD BE OFFERED TO GOD. IF 10% OF THE CATHOLICS IN THE UNITED STATES WOULD PLEDGE TO JOIN THE PERPETUAL ROSARY CRUSADE, SATANIC EVIL WOULD BE CRUSHED IN OUR NATION AND IN THE WORLD.

Please join the Perpetual Rosary Crusade. Pledge ONE HOUR A WEEK! In that hour each week, pledge to pray the 15 decades of the Rosary.

If you will make that sacrifice, you may make this commitment privately; or you may send me your name, address, and the day of the week and hour you have chosen.

Rev. Albert J. M. Shamon
P. O. Box 735
Auburn, NY 13021

"Say the Rosary every day to obtain peace for the world." (Our Lady at Fatima 1917).

"I desire the holy Rosary to be recited often. . .in order to obtain grace and mercy for all." (Our Lady to Fr. Gobbi 6/10/87).

> *Prayer has no sword nor saber,*
> *No mighty bayonet,*
> *Threats not to crush its neighbor*
> *'Neath its heel—and yet*
> *When all else fails, prayer prevails.*

The Fifteen Mysteries of the Rosary

FIVE JOYFUL MYSTERIES
1. The Annunciation
2. The Visitation
3. The Birth of Christ
4. The Presentation
5. The Finding of the Child Jesus in the Temple

FIVE SORROWFUL MYSTERIES
1. The Agony in the Garden
2. The Scourging at the Pillar
3. The Crowning with Thorns
4. The Carrying of the Cross
5. The Crucifixion

FIVE GLORIOUS MYSTERIES
1. The Resurrection
2. The Ascension
3. The Descent of the Holy Spirit
4. The Assumption of Mary into Heaven
5. The Crowning of Mary Queen of Heaven

DAYS ON WHICH THE MYSTERIES ARE RECITED
Monday . . . . . . The Joyful Mysteries
Tuesday . . . . The Sorrowful Mysteries
Wednesday . . . . The Glorious Mysteries
Thursday . . . . . The Joyful Mysteries
Friday . . . . The Sorrowful Mysteries
Saturday . . . . . . The Glorious Mysteries
Sunday . . . . The Glorious Mysteries
                    (Sundays in Advent, Joyful Mysteries; in Lent, Sorrowful Mysteries.)

How to Say the Rosary

9. Concluding Prayers*

Hail, Holy Queen, Mother of Mercy, hail, our life, our sweetness, and our hope! To thee do we cry, poor banished children of Eve; to thee we send up our sighs, mourning and weeping in this vale of tears. Turn, then, most gracious Advocate, thine eyes of mercy towards us, and, after this our exile, show unto us the blessed fruit of thy womb, Jesus. O clement, O pious, O sweet Virgin Mary!

V. Queen of the most Holy Rosary, pray for us:

R. That we may be made worthy of the promises of Christ.

LET US PRAY

O God, whose only begotten Son, by His life, death, and resurrection, has purchased for us the rewards of eternal life, grant, we beseech Thee, that, meditating upon these mysteries of the Holy Rosary of the Blessed Virgin Mary, we may imitate what they contain, and obtain what they promise, through the same Christ, our Lord. Amen.

* These prayers are a fitting conclusion, but are not an essential part of the Holy Rosary.

1. Apostle's Creed
2. "Our Father..."
3. Three "Hail Marys"
4. Announce First Mystery
5. "Our Father..."
6. Ten "Hail Marys" Meditate on the Mystery announced
7. "Glory be to the Father..."
8. Announce Second Mystery and repeat as in 5, 6, 7. Continue in like manner until the Five Mysteries are said.

APOSTLES CREED—I believe in God the Father Almighty, Creator of Heaven and earth; and in Jesus Christ, His only Son, Our Lord; Who was conceived by the Holy Spirit; born of the Virgin Mary; suffered under Pontius Pilate; was crucified, died, and was buried; He descended into Hell; the third day He arose again from the dead; He ascended into Heaven; sits at the right hand of God the Father Almighty; from thence He shall come to judge the living and the dead. I believe in the Holy Spirit; the Holy Catholic Church; the communion of saints; the forgiveness of sins; the resurrection of the body; and life everlasting. Amen.

OUR FATHER—Our Father, Who art in Heaven; hallowed by Thy name; Thy kingdom come; Thy will be done on earth as it is in Heaven. Give us this day our daily bread; and forgive us our trespasses as we forgive those who trespass against us, and lead us not into temptation; but deliver us from evil. Amen.

HAIL MARY—Hail Mary, full of grace, the Lord is with thee; blessed art thou among women, and blessed is the fruit of thy womb, Jesus. Holy Mary, Mother of God, pray for us sinners, now and at the hour of our death. Amen.

GLORIA—Glory be to the Father, and to the Son, and to the Holy Spirit. As it was in the beginning, is now, and ever shall be, world without end. Amen.

OPTIONAL

THE FATIMA PRAYER
(to be said after each decade of the Rosary)

"O my Jesus, forgive us our sins, save us from the fire of Hell, lead all souls to Heaven, especially those most in need of Thy Mercy."

Other Books
By Rev. Albert J. M. Shamon

For additional information, contact THE RIEHLE FOUNDATION, distributor of Catholic Books.

Please write to: THE RIEHLE FOUNDATION
P.O. Box 7
Milford, OH 45150-0007